I0108567

BULL

BULL

THE JOURNEY OF A FREEDOM ICON

Poems

JAMES B. GOLDEN

SILVER BIRCH PRESS
LOS ANGELES, CALIFORNIA

© copyright 2014, James B. Golden

ISBN-13: 978-0615987095

ISBN-10: 0615987095

FIRST EDITION: April 2014

Email: silver@silverbirchpress.com

Web: silverbirchpress.com

Blog: silverbirchpress.wordpress.com

Mailing Address:
Silver Birch Press
P.O. Box 29458
Los Angeles, CA 90029

Cover: (from left) Harry Luther Benjamin, Carolyn Benjamin Folsom, James "Bull" Golden, and Ezell Golden (1955)

Page 2: James "Bull" Golden (1971)

Page 100: James "Bull" Golden and James B. Golden (1989)

To my beautiful nieces
so that you'll always know
Papa was an icon—

Oh Freedom, oh freedom, oh freedom over me
and before I'd be a slave, I'll be buried in my grave
and go home to my Lord, and be free.

CONTENTS

AUTHOR'S NOTE

I can imagine the blood dripping slowly onto the mud beneath the dead man's body...and the smell of sun-stained flesh rotting above the lynch mob...and my grandmother's heartbeat as she unfolds her arms to somehow protect her children from the reality of the Jim Crow American South.

While my grandmother, Henrietta, wasn't actually at the site of Emmett Till's murder on August 28, 1955, there were others like him, especially in South Carolina. The lynching, murder, and castration of Black men prompted the unexplainable disappearances, forgotten funeral services, and bitterness at God. The lynch ropes left unfathomable scars, especially on the young.

I suppose my father, Bull, was one of them.

Those scars resurfaced throughout his life in signature moments. Those recollections are the basis for *BULL: The Journey of a Freedom Icon*.

My father, while flawed, is a representation of what I've always considered the great Black American Man, the old school cat, the Bull. He falls in line with the icons that were raised during one of the most horrific periods in America for people of color.

For me, the process of molding these poems has been evolutionary. I was able to go back to August 1944 and think of the circumstances behind my father's birth. Back then, it was just Henrietta and Bull. That was before she married Chamberlain, and had five other almond-colored babies. He was hers only.

Many of the poems in the *A Rainout in South Carolina* section are stories I've heard from my dad over the years. There was the story of how he lied about his father buying him a T-bone steak (Blue Bonnets & T-Bone Steaks), the one about Henrietta being arrested for bootlegging corn whiskey (By the Mason Jars), and my favorite one about how he almost burned his leg off playing with Cousin Ezell's fireplace (Fireplace Cinders).

The joy of this section, for me, is that I recreated moments that I know affected the trajectory of my dad's life. I imagined what it would be like for Henrietta to watch Bull's birth father disappear like train smoke (A Rainout in South Carolina), the 1946 union of Chamberlain and Henrietta, the moment that Henrietta left her children in Columbia with Cousin Ezell (Mammy Opera), and the mystical day she returned to get her babies (Bull's Escape from South Carolina).

The *What Follows A Rain* section tracks Bull's adulthood, the fights (Bull in Mexico), his association with the Black Panther Party (The Ironed People), his prison sentence (Soledad Prison, Blue Bulls, Paper Moon, Pardon), and the death of four of his younger siblings (What Follows a Rain, Bonnie's Eulogy, Harry).

There are several moments in *BULL* that call upon cyclical familial themes of rape and molestation (Take Me to the Water, Psalms 151), depression (Song of My Daughter, Baby's Gone, Soon I Will Be Done), and unwavering love (Valerie, He Gave Me Records, Mama's Gone).

In many ways, writing this book has been a cleansing of my own soul. I feel more connected to my father than ever, and he's someone I'd want to be connected to forever. As I experienced on the discovery of Rita Dove's *Thomas and Beulah*, the stories of our elders heal our souls. My soul is healing.

Above all, I feel honored to spring from a man whose life has been an iconic guidepost for Black men—all men, really. My dad's tenacity and ability to overcome every hindrance of a pitiless world makes him *Bull*—an unrelenting beast stamping his hooves through many darknesses or, like Emmett Till, a father of many.

James B. Golden
April 2014

BULL

A RAINOUT IN SOUTH CAROLINA

> Take me to the water,
> take me to the water,
> take me to the water,
> to be baptized.
> —*Nina Simone*

OH, MARY DON'T YOU WEEP

I was born in South Carolina between World War II and
    FDR's 4th term
        to the rumbling Model T engines and
        Columbia stillnesses

Helplessly to Henrietta Golden and George Rogers in
    Orangeburg County where
        Eartha Mae Kitt collected train track pebbles.

Smoke laid eggs through our kitchen vent
        sooted nighttime spicy ash from North Auxiliary
        Airfield.

Soldiers lined in rows twirling steel batons in the coolness
        Oh, Martha—don't you moan.

HENRIETTA'S FRONT PORCH

The sun creeps up beneath the window seal
above Henrietta's front porch.

Sizzling eggs fuck to
Billie Holiday's "Don't Explain."
She pops words around the
oak wood South Carolina cabin
lit in between dust speckles
scattered throughout the stale air.

Barefoot country boys, two, smash out
the cracking screen door
leaving shadow footprints on the floorboards.

The hum of a red Studebaker
parks beside the great granddaddy magnolia.

SLAM!

Car doors hide Black men
from sicking bloodhounds
trolling rabidly down Cedar Street,
painting a trail of stamps along the walk.

The hollow creaking of Granny's
rocking chair
eulogizes the Antebellum South.

Back to front
waves break sunshine in the
morning rise.

THE LYNCHING OF EMMETT TILL

There is a dark leaf growing on a Willow.
Mysteriously close to the hull
catkin big as the South—
very straight, with personality,
lacey stingray tails
gibbously pitted circles.

We step fervently to smell the fruit,
carry its branches to Tomb Sweep
the river bed. The moon hums a cathedral
purple glow as Black vultures
descend upon the puddle of sticks and
mud beneath us.

Henrietta's legs go motionless
her arms unfold eagle wide as
glimmers of daylight fade, shine, fade,
shine, speckles in the dead dark forest.

A single American flag
flogs well in kerosene and
ammo scented winds
push in a choral refrain from the Willow,
O babies gather 'round old Uncle Rastus.
No white trash can fool me . . .
there's a nigger in the moon.

We stand
in ruins
as the torch lit Willow leaf
cries down in the Bottom.

Bats, axe handles, crowbars, pale fists
pound the maddened sky
challenge God, scream their pants off
holler for salvation, hoot for justice
another nigger gone

one safer Carolina.

Our feet, pasted gingerly to the ground beneath
lift as the final one abandons the picnic.
We walk down
       walk down the impatient hill
to harvest the Willow.

Two empty cans of gasoline make company
with the body parts unfitting for souvenirs.
The river sings the blues
Here is a fruit for the crows to pluck,
for the rain to gather, for the wind to suck,
for the sun to rot, for the trees to drop...

Each strand of the lynch rope recounted
a memory of this man's last moments:

were his fingers and toes chopped like salad carrots,
fed to the hounds that drug him from the security of
a splintered four post bed at 7:32 p.m.?

Were his teeth withdrawn with auto pliers or
bashed in by sledgehammer?

Did he fight or recall the 1922 anti-lynching bill
or the filibuster that exterminated it?

Was his skin as Black as the licorice jellybeans
Henrietta loved to force on us after
we'd picked the reds and yellows away?

Did he know Civil Rights wouldn't rest by hammock?
That Emmett Till's mangled body would
Cut us down
Cut us down
Cut us down

Did he know that he would cut us down?

24

Cut us down
Cut us down
Cut us down

And the wail released from Henrietta's deep jaw
ends all prayers for freedom.

Henrietta prays a twenty slave prayer,
blesses the head and shoulders
left buried in the Willow,
and continues home.

LITTLE BEE

Butter and charcoal snog the patio ledge
calmed by a last cigarette's smoke
delivering sandalwood from Dionysus
wine stains settled on oak.

Broccoli tops near *mountainscapes*
dive head first into the freshest Bodum-
sliced espresso, and I knew
it was ok.

A RAINOUT IN SOUTH CAROLINA

Surely there is an old musty stagecoach
trotting along somewhere without you.
Rightly so as it should.

You won't stare at 5 young babies
famished from Cream of Wheat suppers, sigh
and churn the lumps out with
a Goodwill hand-me-down brass fork.

Those meals won't worry you much.

*

Your progeny was glad.
Your clip fell not from the block
and bricks stacked themselves built
fifteen feet high outside a vacant patio deck.
But he was less man for you, Henrietta,
hands raised face-close
closed in noose on neck
Bible stamps bleeding on the
oak record player
stuck out glitter glinting from the splinters.
How did your smile stay erect?
We heard death cries from your bedside
water puddles mirrored perfume decanters
the vacancy beside you at night.
That he did not love you enough to
be a man.

*

Dust filled up the sky as
the train to Harlem disappeared in the night.
Under the rained-out stars we prayed
shut our eyes in hushed voices
anticipating a derailed train.

We couldn't hear God for the
clacking of wheels against the tracks.
You dissolved from eyesight
and we stood alone
catching the final bits of dust-rain
in an old mason jar.

*

You took the powder and went forever.

We saluted South Carolina's flag
as the station wagon pulled from the driveway.
Our house no longer belonged
to the aster-clad yarn sofa.
It belongs to some other man's grandson.

Yours won't ever plant a rosebush garden
in memoriam
nor canter in by August stagecoach
to say goodbye to you.

We've already done that.

MOONLIGHT IN THE GHETTO

Light breaks on Washington-Carver Village
but 4 moments each year
when closest to the moon.

We see Black girls Double Dutching
the bleach-stained courtyard lawn
dry desert of the ghetto.

Schoolyard ballets sing poor tunes
yellow flower trumpets smile
cinders float about the room
unit 28 smells of ramen noodles
and spam sandwiches
gripped, eaten quicksand in
sinking adolescent boy stomachs.

Purple Kool-Aid circles seep deeper
in boo boo brown carpets, growing prickles
for patched roach families.

Mice scatter to corner havens
granted sanctuary by cracking plaster
holstered along a broken broomstick.

Baby cries as time bombs erupt
outside the living room nursery window
lodging silver bullets between brick creases.

Home is but a sober figure invisible,
without light, without vision.
Drunken concrete prison
hopelessly chained people.

CHURCH PICNIC

Sister Collier's shepherd ring orbiting milky
lemon-lime straw hat
sashays about the wind
looking migh-tee-fine to the
cherry scarf concealing a patch of
wind-soft chin stubble.

Homemade barbeque sauce sticks to
Deacon Holmes' moustache
just below the grassy nose hairs.

Five Blind Boys of Alabama harmonize
over the potato salad
...above my head I hear music in de air
der must, der must be a God somewhere.

On the other side of Johnson Park,
The Jackson Southernaires battle
Jesus gave me water and
Ah feel like praisin' him
Ah feel like playin' bones!

Dominology, or the study of dominoes,
excites Deacon Loveless who
puts the capital 'D' in every game
where only a fool sits in his seat.

Pastor Davis slides coyly in his sweat suit
trading shoulders on a slow   motion   stroll
thrusting swift anointings
Boom!
        Souls slain
                in the spirit.

Sister Myers turns forearms around as wheels
hoopin' n hollerin' *It's time ta eat!*

Elder Lamb's praying longer than Cary Grant's nose
Thank Ya!!! Thank Ya!!!
Pat down sweating, preaching
Easter Sunday sermons over
the lunch table.
No microphones to grunt at seagulls
making giant clouds in the blue
ready to pounce on Sister Williams'
fried turkey if an *AMEN!* doesn't find
its escape from the long-winded prayer.

Sitting intently picking bones from
Henrietta's ocean-fresh fried catfish
sipping from the rust-dusted spout
the church mourns
beholding the pasty 3-year-old boy
at the water fountain across the park.

TAKE ME TO THE WATER

A meadow sits beneath cherry carpet
chained by box, serenading onlookers
at Gethsemane Baptist Church.

If anyone sees it roar up
the mighty righteous dip and disappear.
Wasted spring water fit for
afternoon skinny dipping imaginary
backyard pool reclining.

Water jumps down by snare upbeat
the bass boom makes dimples in sheets
Sister Williams crinkles her forehead skin
singing "I want to live in a building
not made by hand."

Springboks jump on bushes
stepping Ghanaian Shutterbox Bops
in the pew,

swords slay them cold
laid out worn puppies by the aisle.
A thousand bite-sized cymbals
crash in unison with clothed feet
hopscotching for Jesus.

Sweet potatoes and Pine-Sol reach the vestibule
creeping up for our sacrifices
by nightfall.

Blood swipes the doors
Passovers her screams
the air sucked straw-strong
until silence has its way.

The preacher moans, hums
a tobacco field slave song

settles the belt wrapped tape around his waist
throws handkerchief into a bevy of tears
and fans his pulsing collarbone.

Roar choir,   Roar!
Wade in the water children!

          God, trouble this water!

Trouble
          this water!
Plant my feet, sea deep!
Children!
Wade!
Wade!
Wade!

God's gon' trouble the water.

FOR BLACK CHILDREN WHO HAVE CONSIDERED SUICIDE WHEN THE PROMISED LAND WAS ENUF

A mammy cookie jar
looks down on a
derelict playground and Black children
hopscotch or double-dutch or
play with twenty-twos
practicing soda can targets
against the fence.

The park has dim light,
especially at dusk
they finger their way on
at dinnertime.

We are rich as 7 Up cake
South African minerals
underneath the sun
full of Soweto marching
and early morning burning
lips out like puckering tide foam
eyes big bowling balls,
crystal by night
full of snowy days
instead of sun.

We are captives, blood
can't you see
America's Most Wanted
looks like me.
in search of
liberation's key
remove these rusty chains
from our feet
that we may play in
the sun to our own
drum beat.

BLUE BONNETS & T-BONE STEAKS

Rocks pop at little Black boy feet
dragging along a Gervais St. catwalk.
Little cracker girls switch hippo wide
hips pace mile sides
giant steel science center pendulums.

My daddy bought me a $15 steak—T-bone,
mine hadn't even produced shitty chit'lins.

Your'n daddy ever brought one for y'all?
I was Olympian in the mind, hurdles of memories
a living 1955 gold medal finalist.
Lies rankled between my back teeth grand canyons.

Daddy was the Battle of Saigon
Daddy was the Berlin Blockade
Daddy was Marxist.

I knew Vietnam as noodles and water soup for the wealthy.

I didn't know my daddy
I didn't know my daddy
much less rested eyes upon a steak—T-bone.

A little Black boy drew a profile in the buttery sun
stared ocean-eyed at a dirt starch pressed paisley blue bonnet
Lips, a row of collards
breath-smoke escaping tongue captivity.

Little cracker girl's vaulted right eyebrow
wouldn't let loose, burrowing
a Carolina bastard
under the clouds
under the maples.

The burnished pendulum swung off center
toward First Citizens Bank.

Hey little cracker girl!
My daddy's cost $35—
and we ate that sucker 'til
middle marrow.

THE 1946 UNION OF CHAMBERLAIN & HENRIETTA

The dust broom on church steps
is no champagne cork
to wed a plantation's daughter.
Four envelope folds and Henrietta's
butt make butterflies
train the aisle. The broom
is worship. The broom
clanks offerings for yellowish
wicker baskets at 12:30 p.m.
on Sundays.

Henrietta
in Nigeria would have
crinkled *naira* clothespinned
to kente
hoofin' to a pre-Fela Kuti
cloudburst of drums
pa pa tatui, pa pa tatui.
She doesn't dance a
dance when she's
chicken, at times, fried
inside, squeaking glass notes
through the shadows of death.

It usually readies up the
front porch of Cracker Joe and
Elizabeth Taylor, thorny blistering
coal-walk of Sao Paulo,
ice-slick Antarctic slope,
desolate forest, love-barren
alligator-infested murky swamp
of South Carolina, and
1947 auction block for free men.

The broom believes
it lives upstairs from
'Whites Only' signs and
hog maws settling to chit'lin stew.
Sometimes it plays Lady's
Monday blues, rests for coolness
beneath troubled elm leaves,
where Black mothers go to
mourn their sons, rake pieces of
their fallen fruit from blood sores,
where they pretend to marry
men like Chamberlain.

The broom plays lead tambourine in
Nat Cole's trio, loves for sentimental
reasons. It maintains relation to
Cleopatra, swears its splinters are
Egyptian jewels dug from
Nile sand dunes, believes it
fucked Mark Antony and all
western culture

and in America,
it takes a breath by the
church steps, feels Henrietta's cool rushing
fog above it,
plays her on.

BY THE MASON JARS

Country gin
bathtub beast
stirred with
Henrietta's corn
whiskey

Muddied field pools
in Mississippi ditches
lake clear
translucent molasses

*
Sirens cry through
Columbia's midnight
screeching dust hurricanes
out lorn worn porch

Footsteps
        Footsteps

thundering snares
popping down beat
symphony signals

Mama, what you doin'
on the wall?

Face turns a half moon
metal bracelets crawl
up wrists click clacking
on the sink by the mason jars
lined along the ceiling
A whirlpool tornadoes
the bathtub

Henrietta goes for a ride
through Columbia's November chill

MAMMY OPERA

Purple mice skate barbeque pits through sand.

Jiggling leg strums air guitar.

Giant brown clock on the wall finger snaps.

Black songstresses *operaphize* the kitchen by stove eye.

Mama is gone and God bless the child that sees suns set
in 1955 Columbia smoke clouds.

Mama is a Caravan
etches record grooves in the rain.

'I Loves You Bull' boils Porgy to soup
mixes with Carolina cow milk, chops cane stalks.

Mama is gone by noon.

It's time for tea.

SUNDAY MORNING MAID

Wash the greens
fry the okra
stew tomatoes
peel potatoes
sugar the yams
seer the lamb
brew sweet tea
meringue the lemon pie.

Set the table
pour the maple
syrup the pancakes
                        breathe

short break

wipe sweat from forehead
get kids from bed
dress baby
play Lady
stick butt out in my Sunday gown
run up
            around and blues it
                        down.
Camelwalk it out
ass sit down.

FIREPLACE CINDERS

Last night, my leg beloved
met with Ezell's fireplace.

It preached from the Genesis flood narrative
of raven-hued boys that don't listen.

God gave Noah the rainbow sign
and baptized me in the fire *this* time.

I jitterbugged for him, blessing each room
of the ark parading an Indian infrared glow
through my corduroy chaps.

Four hundred feet high the fire crept up and up
as the cymbals shook water from floodgates
and the heavens opened on my behind.

On the six hundredth year, and seventeenth day of fire
the Columbia voodoo witch doctor severed Comfrey
and talked to the ghost of luminosity
resting like quiet chicken grease over the stove eye
on my right calf.

She blew breath strokes and huffed the
pit brewing on my leg, yes
she wafted and exhaled cigarette
scented suspirations on my leg.
She blew the rainbow on my rolling pin
my chair post
and then my
tail went red.

BULL ESCAPES SOUTH CAROLINA

Pink pillows grow on wooden spoon handles
outside of Ezell's front window,
fogged by burning grits smoke
nose mist and longing for mama.

I escape from my cousin's house
through cloud photos
high-noon iced creamsicles,
her version of Henrietta's coconut cream pie
cooling on a waggling Maytag machine
out back
and the romance of mama thundering in
to Columbia by way of golden carriage
to bring us home.

*

Presley's new ditty steals the fog
makes me hate him
and I hated Elvis Presley
and *Hound Dog* had been Black coffee
in Ezell's kitchen since I was born,
a Bessie already brewed blues pots
between nicotine morning cushions.

Carolyn plays ragdoll by the sycamore.
Bobbie, only 2, already sings the blues
like Big Mama Thornton, howling ace of spades
dark as magic, thrift store guitar
strumming branches.

Harry climbs my post like a Blue Ridge discovery
journey, spilling for me to bring him up   bring him up
to the clouds, above the sheets
above the cordwood cross ablaze in the distance.

I stay looking for a sign,
any, that mama thunders in to Columbia
to save me from Elvis, save us from
the blues.

*

Maybe by dream, the honeyed smell of
gasoline and dust run through my sleeping
eyes, set behind sleep boogers and
tears, Henrietta's hand lays biscuits, dough soft
on my dewy cheek, a brook falling down hers.

The thunder made its praise
I melted fresh Havarti in her arms
as the door behind us
settled uncovered.

MEMPHIS

What Memphis is to me:
the South's spaceship or slick anthill
hole of August ginger and brick brown
anybodys avoiding the evening's temper.
Penniless men steering bicycles to the ghetto
eggplant-bottomed women rolling hair in brick ovens,
rattling, skipping Frankie Lymon & The Teenagers
records, and Doo-Wop makes a home
on every corner.

It is Elvis Presley playing photo time with
Tennessee State Troopers in front of Jerry's Barbershop
on St. Jude Street, as The Diamonds
sha la la la "Why Do Fools Fall in Love" like lukewarm
yogurt attempting to feel-up Mammy's smothered chops,
their silly winces and American Bandstand
children rolling in yard dirt with German Shepherds.

And, it's where a writer said *before Elvis,*
there was nothing. And where *nothing* referred
unwaveringly to the maids brushing bleach dust
from aprons at a mid-street bus stop and
the ice man delivering five hundred plus pounds of
freezing glaciers to every white-only store across town,
where only Black-owned bookstores made
Giovanni's Room front-shelf-worthy
and put Ginsberg in the 'Others' section.

Memphis 1956 displayed photos of
Autherine Lucy alongside *Nigger Bitch* in newspapers
and sold them at the restaurant all seven of us,
because Fair made the 7th, had to saunter
front to mud-covered backyard to grab
doggy bags for our journey west.

It's where I learned The Platters had
no faces in record stores and were

meant to integrate or *cross*over or some
other justified blanching of our skin,
to help whites feel *more comfortable* with
the artists they'd always gotten drunk to
at their Bridge games and dart-throwing
competitions in pissy pool halls.

Simone would say it choked her
scooped her guts soft-serve, sprinkled
coconut flakes and stamped it with a
waffle cone for Pat Boone to taste.

And Memphis,
marble cake with clear fences
dog shit on white vinyl
pale hand slapping a Black woman's face,
is a spaceship
from a place where Black was used only to
polish shoes or streak a toilet.

LITTLE ROCK

Boy wit' purple eyes
walkin' through trees
run nigger run
Klan's gon' get you
betta run.

White hood skins
pretty paper in de breeze
horses pump dirt
maud hooved prints
September wind breathes
lungs beat, chest snares
Little Rock pulses
movie theme cander
dust and a crowd
stampeding the sun

run nigger run
Klan's gon' get you
betta run.

Little boy feet danglin'
mid of de sea
run nigger run
Klan's gon' get you
betta run.

Men caged backyard
cockfights, shackled to vines
chitlins, millct
dripping gruel slides
down toes.

Purple eyes cooked blacken
charred gr'lled cra'klin porkloins
sizzling atop streets.

Faces mashed potatoes and concrete
glistening wine grapes taste faintly lemony.
Carved open, treaded over
glad children's fun

run nigger run
Klan's gon' get you
betta run.

BARSTOW

Going west, Carolyn's Napoleon
blue tie sits cockeyed on her ponytail,

Black-girl-African-naps bright as flashlights
resist the boxing wind
sparring with the front seat.

Chamberlain keeps truckin'
as we jet past the 15 Miles to Barstow sign.

Since he became Sergeant General
he's aimed to stop at every damned base

and we seek sanctuary from puke green
uniforms and the clank of dog tags,

crumpled Budweiser cans, five days of sore asses,
stir-craziness, "Blueberry Hill."

The rearview mirror meets my left eye
with the concern of Israelites in Egypt,

"Bull, when I married your mama"
and the Grand Canyon grows in my stomach

Men had only been forgotten hats
on coffee tables, and named George Rogers

"When I married your mama,
                                  I married you too."

And I have a daddy by Barstow,
not a last name and train smoke

                                        a daddy.

Henrietta clutches the baby still
sawing firewood with her mouth

only the stillness wipes my top-secret tears
and pulls me under its arm.

I love Fats Domino.

940 HARTCOURT AVE.

Seaside, California, salt marsh of western shores,
we kiss at midday Dungeness-crab-oiled
sand-dune-dressed afternoons.

Black vest-pocketed South Carolina family, 5 country
    smothered babies,
bug-eyed, grilled in cotton fields
pebbly tears at first sight of Asilomar
tide pools and 1959 Pontiac windows.

Pacific Ocean, we beseech, roll you like biscuits
kneel in prayer, rock our knees
that the solemnity of Atlantic Ashes won't
desiccate your shores.

Henrietta whines Ella Fitzgerald, Chamberlain
fiddles the blues through muted cigarette,
sea moss and otters praise us
lead us down Broadway
or away from Columbia.

Harcourt is a family's reprint
escape from boiling cotton-picker blisters
drums of corn whiskey
dried spit stains of the crackers
across the railroad track,
and the hum of liberation.

WHAT FOLLOWS A RAIN

BULL

Horns blow clamorously
serenading red carpet
Bull stamps hoof
in the dust cloud.

Steam pours from ear
train-smoke thick
smogging up the air,
nostrils flare.

Bull has been following
ropes all summer
round around
around and round
the ring,

chasing a dream
to prance along the
mountainside with wild
treetop-eating giraffes.

If Bull were man
he'd be stuck at a computer desk
reading Q&A files
overcome with database figures
sea of numbers
waves rolling over
lapping each other
numbers everywhere.

He'd drown in them.

Bull keeps turning circles,
tricks even
nose ring dangling
like a fishing line's bait.

They cast him out
deeper into the rink,
horns go down
matador retreats
he leaps in the stand
snatches a beer in one hand,
a whip in the other
watching Bull
run circles.
Hooves dig,
nose shudders.

THE OLD GUITAR

I cannot find anything up there.
Compositions from the Pacific, the voices
of seaweed.

Only the old guitar.

And Monterey waves are staff
binding and anointing the blues,
fortress, unoccupied and forgotten.

Everything fits up there:
rusted wrist-suffocating handcuffs,
the history-book-thick white cots.

And Monterey waves end when Bull's fingers
drop the acrylic-sopping paintbrush
they've been stroking and dashing
to turn history forward on canvas.

Monterey waves are the ripples on Chamberlain's forehead
propelling the day toward dinnertime.

Or are they tsunamis, destructive beasts?

All other things are missing from there:
illegal guns, Jamaican machetes, a black felt beret.

Everything but the old guitar. And symphony begins

with the first shot
of the revolver, its explosive smoke
lingers on the canvas.

1949 CHEVY

Bull had go.
Go pushing to the joint.
Go far from home, from anklebiters   badasses
and the Salinas Bean Wagons.

Chevy sat softly as new paint patched on a refurbished
hutch mid-Seaside's bone yard.

The Beach Boys didn't make Chevy's cool cat
pimp machines. Feather flappin', flattop funk brothers
stamped chrome panels long before Danny Zuko.

Bull had buzz from the Fuzz
black and whites *wee-o-wee-o-weezin* behind
Black greasers, pre-glassback mufflers,
marching band haulin' ass up Hwy 1.

Broads winced at Chevy's hairy slicks
blew Cherry 7-Up kisses and other things
as the motor revved Bobby Bland.

Bull had hot boxin' cigarettes
a jacked-up front end, jazzed eyes
in rearview, laid scratch
all meat body and moons growing on tires.

His old lady rocked Pacific Grove with Janie
swimming around her abdomen
as the sun set over a
submarine race and a single
kernel of popcorn lodged in the front seat.

BULL IN MEXICO

Because the plush fleece tiger blanket could've swaddled
a baby Nicole or Tiffany as silk
but became the mother's kitchen rag to cool face bruises,
it is likely to be confiscated and sold,

because Black men are arrested for Mexico bar fights
jerking, dancing with handcuffs tightened viciously,
skin goes darker under Mexican moons and
eyes bulge wider than tied up Southern slaves, because

officers have mud-covered skin across the border
darkened by rape and Spain
and no one cares about citizens of the States
who throw blows, even if provoked by red scarf
a tequila challenge, and *nigger*
the first name I can't escape, even in Mexico,

because the stench of Mission camps lives on my skin,
America somehow perspires stronger through pores,
the face bruises bubbling up from iron cell bars
as my presence in Mexico is questioned again
and my snout steams after the *toreo* wins—by default or
longing for a black and orange blanket.

THE IRONED PEOPLE

"...a rose I'll wear to honor you, and when I fall
the rose in hand, you'll be free and I a man"
—Alprentice "Bunchy" Carter

How many
more roses will a casket
hold in 1966
and bury the revolution?

She sits, Denzil Dowell's mother,
the glimmer of Oakland pig badge
in her eyeballs, dry cotton
and a shit-stain-streaked uniform

waiting for revolutionary action
invincibility, and her son's *gaga*
stroll through the tenement door.

Victors write history and we
wear black berets in summer,
not that leather makes herds of
nigger cattle

grazing the Lego black pastures
designed for cows. The revolution
Saran-wrapped our history,
spoiled and had bacteria eat strands,
pulled Ruchell Magee's slight afro
squeezed his brown areola and said
come here Black bitch, let me show you
what we do with pretty niggers!

She makes rocker of a wooden stool
on Grove St. in North Oakland,
where pretty Huey, banana colored
lies patient on a Goodwill tweed sofa.

We shall submit or fight,
a Vietnamese cub tips softly in the store front
Oakland is rice fields
and we brawl.

Bunchy, Bobby mark time by boot click
greased elbows, plastral pilot coats,
grass and Bull's guns— M-14s, M16s,
sawed-off, double-barrel, and magazine shots,
air rifles, needles, submachines, semis,
and Bull's gats.

Bulls guns outfit the West at
7304 E. 14th Ave., East Oakland
3106 Shattuck, Berkeley
2941 35th St., Sacramento
329 W. Meyers, Fresno

Panthers trudge the Amazon
wet leaves, silent indentations in the wind
venturesome cats slinking
grenades, buckshot, gun powder, missiles
torpedoes, shells and Bull's guns
lie caterpillars on spine.

By invincible thought, they bury roses in San Leandro
and we see each other through prison bars:
Angela Davis, Ericka Hudgins, George Jackson
John Cluchette, Fleeta Drumgo, and Bull
only seen by silhouette or the moon,
prisoners where Black is already prison.

Pigs enslave the ironed people
jostle feeders down their throats
and hoot *Like it nigger bitch*
suck it, suck fascisms nuts,
suck on Elvis!

And Aretha sends code

If you see me walking down the street
and I start to cry...
walk on by
walk on by
make believe you see the dazzlingly
muddy skin of Carolina Rice pickers.

Baneful huntress eyes call
pigs fat as chit'lin lining
or slaughtered hogs
and save our tears in coffins
for roses or 3 AM prison pillows.

SOLEDAD PRISON

Eyes burn holes through water plastic windshields at Soledad
Prison
     Red as Mars droppings fleeing space.
You're my son no longer, the marshmallow moon has risen.

Speed cars machete winds, dust looms capped behind engine,
     Siren lights the diving backdrop, in place.
Eyes burn holes through water plastic windshields at
     Soledad Prison

Told grass sold limitedly Black boy's excursion fishing
     Mama knew guns guns guns grew in tackle boxes as
     bait,
You're my son no longer, the marshmallow moon has risen.

Night lastly births the darker sky hued cinnamon
     Deception leaves Ajax stains on living room couch
     lace
Eyes burn holes through water plastic windshields at
     Soledad Prison

This, then, becomes a father's brim tip before the fate of
     animism
     That Joshua cried the cry, danced the dance of disgrace
You're my son no longer, the marshmallow moon has risen.

Fingers reach for Kleenexes, dab off the remnants of blood
     after crucifixion
     A sullen pocket-watch ticks briefly between the
     Samsonite corner-pocketed briefcase

Eyes burn holes through water plastic windshields at
     Soledad Prison
You're my son no longer, the marshmallow moon has risen.

BLUE BULLS

I am an alcoholic without shame.

The sun lights my Marlboros
time is my hairbrush.

Every bull is a victim of the blues, *too*.

>Crystal decanter pourin'
>>.22 burned on my thigh

>Crystal decanter a pourin'
>>.22 burned on my thigh

>Dirt green cot center stage in cement and me
>alone with the night.

>Blood done beat me pink
>>stripped my tongue, snatched my teeth

>Blood went and beat me down to pink
>>funked my words and snatched my teeth

>Need a lighter and seven dollars, just to cry
>me home to sleep.

>The night calls liquor mirrors
>>raindrops basting on my cheeks

>The night calls liquor mirrors
>>raindrops, Morton's flavored, down my cheeks

>Take this rain-soaked skin, burn the sun
>beneath my feet.

Bull sings the blues
　　　men burned by suns always do

A bull sings his blues
　　　every Black boy burned by suns always do

Jack irons the soul
　　　until the bottle bursts me through.

PAPER MOON

I wish the smoke wouldn't
cut on my fingertips
or that beer-filled wineglasses
aren't medicinal on lonely nights.

I plea that the temporary happinesses
exist not only in dramas,
and leading characters don't believe death
an apt means to wholeness.

The elm tree contours have purpose
on Wednesday evenings,
a man is just a shadow in time's nightcap,
John Coltrane isn't the balm on brokenness
and cigarettes don't fill the lungs of the empty.
Tomorrow is already a waste of misery
the brokenhearted linger in its tail.

The bass jumps falling on floor,
chord progressions slow heartbeat
to flat time symphony.

The shit-colored roach crawls beneath
an abandoned couch, hidden from civilization.
The empty wishes he were a roach,
whose life is less about fucking and leaving,
more about surviving the cold ashen air.

The Coors Light seeps darkness to veins,
stares fear down with AK47 eyes.

I am paper moon in torched clouds

concerned life won't stay a friend,
it will pass a cold sore.
smoke drifts further away.

SOLEDAD PRISON 2

"Don't worry about a thing…"
—Bob Marley

As no one eats
Christmas cookies alone,
neither caged autonomously
nor as eagle,
certainly against tradition
snapping them each
Henrietta's Sunday peas
in half

frail as twig arms
sausage fingers rolled too thin
dipped in red sugar glitter
glinting freedom's lamplight.
Sterile bed sheets fill with crumbs
stressed Pruno blotches fail
remnants of slopped Soledad Champagne
color the chalk tallies above the toilet
and three tree swallows keep company
on the carroty rusted windowsill.

PARDON

He's kneaded his muslin necktie twice
and pace marched into the courtroom. From the gallery
with its city slick Stacy Adams, log-built church pews,
Henrietta gazes upon a hand of chocolate Jell-O.

Before Soledad, Bull vowed to sit for Janie.
He was half-grown then, a brute
whose fit raged on sight of even beets
flushed pink by sunlight. In the room

the black robe swishes and mocks the flag.
She occupies the stairwell,
resigned to careful prayers or clement,
waiting for her son to follow.

SEASIDE BLUES

A mother sits at the
laundromat,
baby in tow
waiting for the spin cycle
to unload her clothes.

Outside a bum
lies awake staring down
the sun
waging war against
the weather gods
against the inferno
below.

The sun beams down on
a grandfather's Jetta
peering through the sunroof
bona fide peeping tom
resting forehead rays
on a mother's baby
trapped by car seat
screaming *Help!*

No one hears but
Rolled-up window creases in
double-paned glass,
the expensive kind
found only on foreign
automobiles.

The washer machine
says *buzz*
the bum hums
and baby's silent
cooing in her sleep.

PISS & TEARS (OR LETTERS TO THE UNBORN CHILD)

Day 1

Her guts are on the toilet seat
just above praying knees and an EPT pen.
The flood of a thousand Louisiana's lifts up
eyelids and she begins to pour.

How does a jellybean grow inside a pussy?
These arms are not strong enough to lift
love through another being.
And even if you love me now,
will you still love me tomorrow?

Day 2

Clinics smell like mustard and funk.
Who eats a fucking hot dog in Planned Parenthood?
All these brown girls dart eyes
judging us for handling you.
She cannot bear nine months of unhappiness
resentment at the man who
stuck his penis in and infected a body.
She was already whole without you.

Never knew I could hate something sweetly
a part of me, Jellybean.

> *As I lay, nighttime prays*
> *As I lay, ancestors pray*
> As I lay, the pimp Black bastard prays

Pray there's a heaven for jellybeans.
Let them pop on gingerbread houses
iced with stratus clouds.
Let them sing, even Elvis.

But,
let them.

Plastic snakes slither in,
breaking her home.
She goes in whole to
leave alone.

Day 3

If beds could talk, mine would shout
teary Kleenexes land on sheets. Crap
and blood droplets turn white
a filthy meth color.

Queens don't lie in their piss and tears
royal bodily sacraments.
Where is her crown, throne of happiness?

And if darkness is lit by the moon,
where are her stars?
I killed starlight.

Fifteen or thousands of prayers resurrected from this
bed cross: that you will love me still, even though
I couldn't take care of you,

that you'll remember my lilacs in heaven,
that you'll love me tomorrow.

PSALMS 151: FOR VICTIMS OF RAPE

1 There was no one to rescue her,
though her scream was a slaughtered
Zebra in the Kalahari.

2 The congregation's praises drowned in
the wilderness, the girl found in the country
screamed, but there was no one to
rescue her.

3 Shange says *a friend is hard to press
charges against, if you know him*,
but what of a pastor, God's anointed,
who will rescue her?

4 Who, if she is 6, will deliver her on
Sunday morning, keep her from using
the bathroom and getting raped
by crucifix?

5 If a girl is found slain, lying
in a field in the Land of the Lord your God,
she is tied up by two big Black tree trunks,
shame, and not wanting her mother to die

at the hands of a rapist who
everyone knows. *6* If she does not please
the master who has selected her virgin
vagina for himself, she is ungodly and no less

worthy of forgiveness than Mary Magdalene.
7 Black girls are a commandment in
churches that make them cover legs with
nylon and sit far   *8* stay far away from the pulpit.

9 Loneliness is a refuge for scarred virgins,
those without a voice to scream in the
country. *10* Jordan is Dinah violated by her
son and given away as a Christmas fir with
sparse branches.

11 Daughters, in their preciousness, remain silent
when having a wooden cross shoved up
their asshole mid-service. *12* Parents continue
praising, blindly, eager to raise Dove pure girls

while   *13* they are raped
in church bathrooms
by faith.

WELLINGTON SMITH JUVENILE HALL

Mothers line in field crop rows to bury
children in Salinas desperateness; they say their boys
are Cain without fathers, "spirits that would rather kill
than hope he'd return with a threadbare cross," they say.
The adobe, mothers say, comfort them
long walks through thorn stems and torched coals
to bury baby boys in halls of resistance or concrete.
I believe they sing sparrow melodies to the sky,
but can't rely on Ai poems about motherhood and snakes:
"They say I'm protected from harm because the Virgin Mary
put her heal upon the snake's head"; I would
agree until snakes slither into the halls, covering
floors beneath the children I serve,
laying eggs as mothers do, even in desert heat.
Ave Maria, mothers sing, and Mary
doesn't exist for them.

SONG OF MY DAUGHTER

Maud stands tamed in the kitchen
the stare of death cutting across the room.
Here, 3 steps from the front doorknob
reddened, hot as fried rabbit in peanut oil
Baby Girl clung to the brown leather *James* belt
buckle from Tijuana.

Seaside escapes outside, into the velvet
pint-smoke filled night.
Lemonade-colored Baby Girl asks the heaven of stars
to keep Daddy from slamming the door,
escaping his past.

Amputated lampshades and strewn records
live along on the Play-Doh den carpet.
She asks the wharf to keep him occupied
with paints long enough that he'd cook
dinner tonight instead,
that his daughters wouldn't remain fatherless
long.

Silence in Seaside.

The docks forget a baby's prayer,
carrying him on a Sunday freeway.
Don 't leave me, Daddy,
please don't leave me...
not on a Sunday.

Baby Girl's tiny body jerks and spasms as
her face glows with freshly escaping
confined tears filling the pink beach house sink.
She brushes Malibu Christie's hair, purring lullabies
Sit there and count your little fingers . . .
all you can ever count on
are the raindrops . . .

No one hears her song, the dead girl,
and she lies moaning all afternoon.

BABY'S GONE

The lights are out
forgot to pay again,
sink's filled with dirty dishes
baby's clothes floor scattered
feet demand clubbing
I left an accident in the oven
burnt butter grows stronger on carpets
mixed with charm
and chocolate.

My baby's gone
with my baby
booked a night trip to Oakland
the half-slip sits still
on bathroom counter
26 days later and
4 hours.

I FEEL LIKE PRAISIN' PRAISIN' HIM

"Before I sing I must feel"
—Ira Sankey

Praise him in the morning
    the winter
    and testimony

Praise him in mourning
    on Bull's testimony
    of the winter

Praise him this morning
    for the winter
    or testimony

If you don't wanna shout
don't bother me
creep in as harmony, weepy baritone, a
Fisk Jubilee symphony, arranged on
the voices of the Darker Place
Thomas A. Dorsey's antenna fingertips and
tambourine cymbal nails.
Be dust in a chance wind
in some place that hasn't entombed
the sacred testimony of slave winters.

The holy ghost that I have
the world didn't give it to me
by call and response or chain gang
work songs, Dixie Humingbirds' ballads
or Shirley Caesar tunes.

The blood that gives me strength
lives snow-capped in a South Carolina ditch
at Gethsemane
over 6 unmarked barrows, the
forfeited grub hoe,

79

muskroot from Mary's alabaster jar
the spoiled tapestry of Hammond minstrelsy,
and him.

MOSS LANDING BEACH

A giant log sits beneath my butt
the sun squints my eyes
and the buzz of a sounding horn
pierces the lapping waves.

Two dogs traipse the shore
chasing seagulls through wind.
Brown children splash water in
parent eyes, singing lullabies
in Spanish.

My Vans flood with sand
turn Black brown.

This is what humanity is made of.
One with the Pacific.

We live, multiply, and die
as the shore surely hides us
in the sunset.

Our feet aren't meant for shoes.

VALERIE

I.

I suck oysters for loneliness and pain.
They usually help
beat rhythm back in my chest
sit across a vintage desk with retro glasses on.

Each revelation I fall into
leads me to the South Bend corn stalks,
Anita Baker's *Rapture* album,
and I know nothing at all

of Greyhounds. How they
run from white-sheet-covered bodies. How they are Moses at
the Red Sea. How they hum
toward California at 3 AM.

II.

Seeing the newspaper-colored mountains
dip uncertainly on your bottom lip, retreat and
fall is like catching a 15-pound catfish
and Henrietta dropping it, a ballet in grease.

The cat swims out of the ocean,
zips up patent leather boots, and
does the Hustle with cornmeal under
kitchen ceiling spotlight.

The thought of you eating oysters raw,
a loose wet body, slithering water
snake in lemon juice and hot sauce
makes me love you, today even more.

III.

Sometimes you'd just watch and smile,
eat all the calamari on my plate,
revel in the quietness of kidless enchantment
or pretend chicken nuggets were on half-shell
in hard times.

Sometimes you'd leave mid-night,
with two boys in a cherry-red 1987 Nissan Sentra
and call with, *I still love you Bull but
something's got to change.*

I'd cry at God's moon,
curse the stars for the scars
of South Carolina Black children and
damn the bull within.

IV.

She still loves me for the grizzly
beard, my record collection and ease;
and I know she loves me even harder
for eating oysters.

DREAM IN SUNLIGHT

Bobbie cooks.
I always watched her cook
then grab her wooden cane.

Sugar first layered in Land-O-Lakes
domes popping up from cast iron
skillets whistle I Say A Little Prayer
for you
Dionne simmers by the spinner.

Pineapple Upside Down cakes aren't cooked
by cooks anymore
and Bobbie cooks.

A bull spears meat
African sharp, says
in the matter of barbeque sauce
only Columbia Honey and
coke dust will do.

Pill bottles turn water to orange juice
make citrus candy of disease
line the kitchen window seal
while Bobbie cooks.

Cinnamon, vanilla and lemon extracts,
3 eggs, 3 cups flour, brown sugar,
1 can of only Dole pineapple, a song
maraschino cherries beaten housewife
thoroughly.

Just at *forever and ever you'll stay
in my heart*,
the memory is ready for baking.
I always watched her cook
the way I've always cooked.

A dream embossed in sunlight
kissed on the lips of time
broken as the old wooden cane
and a bull's heart.

THE PETAL-MAKER

This skin is not ours
it belongs to the petal-maker above.

Now it is Spring and the unfolded tulips rise
and the graves grow deeper into the earth.

The grapes settle, great nestled pecans
entombing themselves among earthworms.

And it is time to wave flag, tip the giant hat
run through cloudy hallways, skulk off
the radar
as the flat line runs.

WHAT FOLLOWS A RAIN (BOBBIE)

What follows a rain
but silken misty air and
spikes of coolness.

To what purpose, Seaside wind, do you return again?
You will no longer reside on a place where Bobbie Jean had life.

I know nothing of love anymore.
Love died in the Maryland April snowfall.
It is inconceivable that living is heartache.
Death remains not only underground,
but in the turn of Fall
wind caresses broken leaves along the airwaves.

Life alone
is nothing
a stringless piano, an empty teacup.
Grief comes like an idiot,
sits on the other side of a rain.

BONNIE'S EULOGY

Brothers and sisters, we
have gathered here for
the misunderstood, the
caged orca, and Nina
Simone.

She was Aretha on the
252nd performance of 1968,
Claudine in Rupert's bathtub
before KFC with a baby rat,
a dust-ridden chalkboard.
Tired of tires spinning her veins
pounding up mountains inside her
ovaries, nightfall over Oakland
and hospital hallways with
smiling rainbow children and streaks
of skittles on RN scrubs.

What the fuck was there to
taste but disease's salty balls
and lemon-lime Gatorade, the
flavor that wouldn't taste like
a kindergarten Capri Sun.

Was she expected to wrap Medusa's
snakes around her dome, walk away
from the shimmering Black girl naps
in the bathroom sink and sing
Hallelujah, my face has finally sunken?

Maybe some of you believe she
wasn't strong enough, that
Jesus' nails paid for cancer treatment fees,
but her cross was titanium
and bigger than daydreams.
She belongs to the wind now
and the Pacific.

HARRY

Lungs scar up nasty mountains and
death is inevitable,
as in a loveless marriage.
The Oakland Metro driver dies.

He does not linger long in a hospital bed,
imposing the severance,
jumpstarting bereavement.

A brother's death is final and pure,
as in a sunset,
when the last purply line disappears from the sky.

I only have one brother now,
only one brother.

When the last purply line disappears and,
above the clouds,
the stars crop up, in spite of,
the morning sun.

Soon I Will Be Done

And nobody wants to outlive four
younger siblings enough
to wave American flags
in a cemetery or jump
bones from shoes
as smoke lingers by rifle cannon.

Tumbleweeds pass along
on the road home.
Flesh-scented Columbia Elms
drop decayed fruit to a
side-line ditch along the Saluda.

Nobody want to live beyond
babies they maneuvered away from
whites only placards
and Jim's shitty breath.

And I will be done when mottled
Monterey sanddabs retreat
to crustacean restaurant tide pools
where ashes from the bodies of ones loved
spread as seeping cigarette smoke
in the apartment beneath us.

Nobody wants to live in peace-less-ness
where Whitney Houston records are heard only
in abandoned elevators and
sea urchins gladly flit into
William Sonoma copper paellas.

And I will be done
when the troubles of being me go
numb from Jameson abysses, and
the hums of church mothers gyrate in pews.
I'm going home
to be with God.

HE GAVE ME RECORDS

Latch locked over a pewter plastic case
spindles crank Amtrak loud
Aretha dusts up the room
with wet tile walls
Ain't No Way chokes us dead.

He gave me
strawberry-scented First Sunday sacraments,
The Body & Blood of jazz singers
with the right to sing the blues
chopping a sentimental mood.

He gave me *love the lie and lie the love*
of old women kissing mutts in their front seats,
treasonous Les McCann on wax
popping a left hook to the
vanilla white establishment via
something real compared to what.

Something doo-doo brown, falling from
a Black boy's shot of rum
stuck like a shit log floating toilet reefs.
    Back
          forth
up
down memories dropping
against my window, basting recollections of rain
showers staring back from my windowpane.
He gave me Ann Peebles, I couldn't stand the rain.

He said, "Son, don't waste your time" on
simple silly girls. Get up from your knees
put on War and smoke the sea.
Let it shoot your lungs, plate high
let them sing the expanding balloon ballad.
Force darkness to flee away like dawn does night
windsurf the clouds on a natural high.

But whatever you do, don't waste your time.

Sit patiently to dock, crossing the bridge on stilts
in the morning sun. Watch ships roll in
with Otis, watch them roll away again.

He told me Etta Jones could scrape a splattered soul
from kitchen tiles and sprinkle it on
fried green tomatoes. Salt and cornmeal in grease
dripping love on a paper towel. There wouldn't
be a need to go to strangers.

He gave me home after the love had gone
a palace of records to give my soul pause
a plow to dig the hope from a turnip garden
a stylus to pinch my worries.
He gave me soul.

THE LAKE CALLS YOU HOME

Daddy,
did you forget to tie up the boat?

Your shadow outlines the sunset
rushing over Hunter Ligget.
Packed sandwiches and mustard sardines
Budweiser coolers and Ritz crackers—
preparations for legend at sea.

Daddy steered boats along rocky Asilomar shores,
Vietnam, South Carolina backwaters,
catching bass with stripes and silver catfish
baited hooks
saving souls in winter.

Tell us the story, Daddy
once more
before you rush to a home
promised over Jordan.

Tell us the story of plowing cotton fields
to send your brothers off to college
while you stayed behind to support the family.

Tell us of meeting Henrietta
and raising a slew of children and
grandchildren and great-grandchildren
through the Jim Crow American South.

Tell us of the moment you
walked the planks
approaching a new America,
post-Holocaust.

Tell us of purple hearts and
blood-stained fingernails
barbequing ribs on a garbage can grill.

Tell us your fingers were
sore, picking backyard garden greens
digging up turnips & potatoes,

blasting Five Blind Boys and
Donny Hathaway records.

He would sing *someday we'll all be free*
and you'd believe him.

We believed equally in you, Daddy,
especially by daylight, and certainly in boats.

We believed you knew every single one
of our birthdays and anniversaries like
the hoops on your neck.

Our kitchen cabinets were stocked full
with Daddy's Care Packages.
Lay's and Grandma's oatmeal raisin cookies
overflowing brown paper bag.

Your grandchildren loved you for that
for riding in a fisherman's boat
no umbrellas or lifejackets necessary.

And our hearts beat the mourning drums
along the coast.

The lake calls you home
where all things begin
after the tumultuous rains of disease.

Daddy, it snows in Seaside today
and the waters are colder.
Take comfort in knowing the sun
will shine again but tomorrow.

Daddy, don't forget we loved you.

Don't you dare forget we loved you.

Make salmon and rice for Bobbie,
but without bones.
Play Scott-Heron records for Harry and Bonnie.
Shoot plates with Fair.

Lounge those spider Black legs
on pillows in the
greatest Seaside Fisherman's
boat.

Float away into the sunset,
wave as you move along
when you get a chance,
send us a smile by sunshine
the lake calls you home.

Daddy,
did you forget to tie up the boat?

PEOPLE OF THE SUN

I leave you this
fraction of a poem
stained by bloody words
and picturesque memories.
Consistency in language
and thunderous lyrical cadence.

Nappier hair
big wide nostrils
hopefully dreadful eyes,
a smile longer than the
Golden Gate.

I leave you this
measurement of manhood
manifesto on work ethic
beating the rains like factory workers
in a Cannery Row sardine plant.

Subtly in the clearest form,
depictions of beautiful people of
all skin colors,
carefully woven quilt
some silks   some rayon
soft, resolute to the core.

I leave you this
large town filled with
people of the sun,
those remembered as
unwearying ones.

Steady and planted
like a tree by the waters.

Life and words,
I leave you this.

MAMA'S GONE

One of these mornings
it won't be long,
you'll look for me, and I'll be
gone.

The phone sits patiently, still as
Henrietta's wrists. After noon our
periwinkle hummingbird confused dips
its head to see time drift past.

Minutes drag through the future and
"none but the righteous shall see
God . . ." chokes a moment of oneness.
I am half an egg, curled in a
mother's embrace, longsuffering for deliverance.

I stare at the hummingbird's fatigue
wondering if the Pacific grew in his
stomach as he left Mama. Was
his nest on Hartcourt Avenue or the South Carolina
front porch by which snow was longed for
in November? Was his daddy a mouthful of
Columbia dust?

I wonder if hummingbirds go to heaven,
despite hard lives, even if too easy to matter.
The pulse calls me to watch
West African women burn feet
on hot red clay and smile at the gods
teasing rainclouds overhead.

I lay out photographs of Henrietta.
I remember how her coconut cream pies
made love with our Christmases, how
they were our only presents one year,
and as long as there was coconut, we knew
we had something, anything.

I close my eyes, tight as the blind,
breathe in mama's breath, and
pull out her heart, hold it to my face
kiss it over and over the final moments,
lay on her chest, praying for one more
beat, to say
thank you
thank you
mama

and the tears don't come
as the hummingbird tizzies circles
outside the window, marking the pattern
of time, the passing of a generation.

I hold a lump in my palms
on the walk home, but not
home as I've always known it;
that is *gone*.
I can't go back. I won't go back.
I never left.

CHRONOLOGY

1929: Henrietta Golson-Golden born in Lexington County, South Carolina.

1944: Bull born in Columbia, South Carolina to Henrietta and George Rogers.

1946: Henrietta and Chamberlain Benjamin married. Carolyn born in Columbia.

1947: Harry born in Columbia to Henrietta and Chamberlain.

1953: Bobbie born in Columbia.

1954: Henrietta arrested for illegal alcohol sales.

1955: Henrietta leaves Columbia to meet Chamberlain in Ft. Ord, California. Bull, Carolyn, Harry, Bobbie are left with first cousin Ezell in Columbia.

1956: Henrietta and Chamberlain return to Columbia to bring their children back to Seaside, California. Chamberlain Jr. (Fair) born in Ft. Ord.

1957: Henrietta starts working at Hopkins Marine Biology Lab in Pacific Grove, California, as a glassware cleaner in 1957. Bull starts smoking.

1959: Henrietta buys first car (1959 Pontiac). Bull buys first car (1949 Chevrolet).

1963: Janie born in Ft. Ord.

1966: Bull enters Soledad Prison.

1970 January 5: Bull released from Soledad Prison.

1971: Bull meets Audrey and Desma.

1973: Nicole born to Bull and Audrey in Seaside.

1974: Tiffany born to Bull and Audrey in Seaside.

1976: October wedding in Reno, Nevada.

1977: Elvis dies.

1981: Bull and Audrey separate.

1983: Bull meets Valerie and Samson.

1984: Bull becomes member of Mt. Nebo Baptist Church in Salinas, California.

1985: James born in Salinas to Bull and Valerie.

1987: Bull becomes a deacon at Mt. Nebo. Henrietta retires from Hopkins.

1992: December wedding.

1996, April: Bobbie dies.

1998, July: Bull eulogizes his sister-in-law, Harry's wife, Bonnie. Bull retires from Wellington Smith Juvenile Hall.

2006, June: Harry dies.

2011, January: Fair dies.

2013, February: Chamberlain dies. **March:** Henrietta dies.

ACKNOWLEDGMENTS

Gratitude is given to the City of Salinas for recognizing and trusting a young Black man with the challenge of representing a truly original American literary hub. In that same vein, a special thanks to John Steinbeck for leading the path for Monterey County, California, and American writers to gain a platform to address concerns of the people.

Thank you to all of the publications that have featured the author's work: *The Hip Hop Think Tank, Kapu-Sens Literary Magazine, Vibe, Clutch, Bandersnatch, Jazz Times, The Salinas Californian,* and *The Monterey County Herald,* among others.

Our deepest appreciation goes out to Poet Laureates around the country, including U.S. Poet Laureate Natasha Trethewey, California Poet Laureate Juan Felipe Herrera, and Los Angeles Poet Laureate Eloise Klein Healy. The author also wishes to thank Silver Birch Press for choosing to publish such a provocative work of art. Certainly, this book was inspired early on by the dynamic Rita Dove's seminal Pulitzer Prize winning masterpiece, *Thomas and Beulah.*

#TeamGolden has been instrumental in the promotion and distribution of *BULL.* Thank you Misha Lightner, Tashiana Jefferson, Carrington Baber, Micheal Jackson, and everyone who has worked on our team. The author also wishes to thank all family members and friends, especially for the incredible stories.

A sincerest thanks goes to Nikki Giovanni, who has continued to be an inspiration and poetic mother for the author. Her words of encouragement and thoughtfulness this past year have pushed the author to "keep on keepin' on."

Lastly, thank you Bull Golden for giving us the gift of your story and the ability to *tell it like it T-I is.* You are our freedom icon.

ABOUT THE AUTHOR

James B. Golden was born and raised in Salinas, California, and received his M.P.A. and B.A. in English and Pan-African Studies Arts & Literature from California State University, Northridge. He has edited *Kapu-Sens Literary Journal* and the *Hip Hop Think Tank Journal*. He is the author of *The Inside of an Orange, Sweet Potato Pie Underneath The Sun's Broiler*, and 2012 NAACP Image Award Winner *Afro Clouds & Nappy Rain*. He currently lives in Los Angeles, where he is a freelance music journalist. His articles have appeared in such periodicals as *Vibe, The Root, Clutch Magazine, Jazz Times*, and *Los Angeles Our Weekly*. Golden is the inaugural Poet Laureate of Salinas, California.

www.ingramcontent.com/pod-product-compliance
Lightning Source LLC
Chambersburg PA
CBHW072042040426
42447CB00012BB/2977